Life after Lock-Up

Your Blueprint for Hope After Incarceration

Written by Jennifer A. Rosa

Life after Lockup
Your Blueprint for Hope After Incarceration
Copyright © 2020 by Jennifer A. Rosa

ISBN 978-0-578-82163-4
All scriptures are from www.BibleGateway.com

Dedication

I would like to dedicate this book to you. I hope this book helps you find freedom. It is possible for you to create a unique experience of internal freedom. You can get out of the habits and decisions that may have led you behind bars. Jeremiah 29:11 says "For I know the plans I have for you," declares the LORD, "plans to prosper you and not to harm you, plans to give you hope and a future." The tools contained in this book are intended to provide a blueprint for you, so you can be successful.

Romans 15:13 says "May the God of hope fill you with all joy and peace as you trust in him, so that you may overflow with hope by the power of the Holy Spirit." I pray you accept and welcome the intention of this book. It is never too late to change. You can do this! I believe in you. Take the first step today.

Acknowledgment

I have to start by thanking God, for preparing me for divine destiny and purpose, for His will in my life to be executed. Thank you, Lord, for never giving up on me! Galatians 6:9 says, "Let us not grow weary in doing good, for at the proper time, we will reap a harvest if we do not give up." Also, my mentor and prayer partner, Apostle Dr. Melissa Weathersby, for inspiring me to write this book. I thank God for positioning her at the right time in my life. Her ministry is to encourage and help those who are going through a rough time. As a biblical teacher, she has taught me the foundation of biblical principles and how to incorporate them in my daily life. Thank you for believing in me.

Contents

Foreword

My name is Mel Novak, and I am blessed and honored to write a Foreword for an excellent and anointed book by Jennifer Rosa. I have known Jennifer for 7 years. A friend brought her to my Bible Study that I have taught for 39 years. I watched Jennifer grow in the Lord Jesus Christ and had spent time mentoring her, teaching her about Spiritual Warfare. I gave her my "Arsenal Warfare Prayer" that you can download from my website www.melnovak.com... over a million people have it.

Jennifer learned how important it is to dress DAILY with the Full Armor of God, which is a command. (Ephesians 6:10-17) to increase her prayer time and praise time. Then she knew how to protect her mind from the devil's assaults...the mind is his playground. She started feeling better about herself, knowing God's forgiveness and His love is awesome. As the years went on, I encouraged her to ask God what her calling was. (Psalm 32:8) I had taken her with others from my Bible Study to Skid Row, where I have ministered for 38 years. Skid Row is a prison without bars. She knew I also had a Prison Ministry for 37 years in some of the worst prisons in our country. That is where God put it on her heart to minister in the jails or prisons...to give testimony of how He delivered her through Jesus Christ. We are all called to serve. (Matthew 20:28 and Mark 10:45). She has done this and heeded her calling which unfortunately too many do. She stopped judging herself for her past knowing she is a Child of God...it is Grace.... (Ephesians 2:8) She embraced Matthew 6:33...God has to be FIRST. He gave her wisdom. (James 1:5) I am blessed to see where God has brought her and is taking her. She saw that no matter what success you have in the world, I put God and my

7

calling first. I have starred or Co-starred in 57 Motion Pictures...but led well over 250,000 to the Lord...and have done over 10,000 services "behind enemy lines." GOD IS GOOD!!! Amen...

Introduction

According to statistics from The Unites States Department of Justice, more than 600,000 prisoners are released every year and it is believed that two out of three former prisoners will be arrested again within three years. For me, I have experienced both physical and mental incarceration, and I have come to understand that one does not have to be in prison physically before being incarcerated. With some of the lessons I have learnt, I have been able to create simple tools to help you move forward with your life, regardless of where you may be right now. I want to give you a sense of hope and make you understand that your life is not over yet. Even though you might have made some mistakes, I want you to know that your mistakes don't define you. Your life has just begun, and your best yet to come. This book will also help you understand and use the tools and resources provided to **GET AHEAD**.

My Life

It's a cold winter day. I am sitting in front of my computer, waiting for my friend's phone call. I am starting to imagine the surprises the year still has in store for me. All the possibilities and opportunities that are in front of me seem endless. Bouncing back big in 2020 was my dream and I had been looking unto it which much enthusiasm. Yet with all the possibilities I saw ahead of me, fear was starting to set in. I know I need to take that leap of faith and let God's hand guide me, but rather than leave it all to God, I am starting to feel fearful of the future. I am looking at my current situation and focusing on the problems. My communication with my husband needs improvement. My kids are going through teenage irritability, moodiness, and are basically throwing tantrums. My oldest son seems very distant and unforgiving. I don't blame him; I know I have not been the best mother to him. My bank account is at $0, and my part-time job doesn't pay much. I can't even register for school because I owe the school. I just received a pay or quit letter regarding my rent. I have two amazing dogs that are currently sick, and one of them is going through doctors' appointments while the other one is clinging for its life. Life can be harsh sometimes.

Life is not perfect. There will be rough seasons in our lives, but we have a choice to trust God or not. For me, I choose to trust God in this season, **I DECLARE EPHESIANS 3:20 over my life. God will do exceedingly, abundantly above all that I ask or think**. Even though I am going through the storm, my FAITH will not be shaken because my anchor is Jesus. I am going to praise and thank Him, rather than complain. I am going to thank him for good health, for having a roof over my head, and food on the table. In other places in the world, some people don't even have those three essentials.

Early childhood

The best way to stop thinking about what is bothering me is to share my life experiences with others. I was born Friday, May 10, 1974 in Los Angeles, California and I am the oldest of three siblings. My parents are industrious and committed people who devoted themselves to their jobs. Due to the nature of their jobs, they were not really there to raise me. I was raised by babysitters and maids. I felt neglected from the time I was born, as I was being passed around, from one babysitter to another. I did not have any close connection with my mother and father. I felt like I was in the foster system, and I did not really know who I was. I remember my mother telling me that she had a dream about me crying in the womb. I wonder what that meant. Could it be that my inner soul knew I was going to have a rough start and that my childhood wasn't going to be easy? Starting from a very tender age, I was already being touched inappropriately by people who took care of me. I remember going outside and playing hide and seek with the kids in the apartment building. I remember hiding with a boy who started touching me in inappropriate places, my breast, my behind, sticking his fingers in places that made me feel uncomfortable. I was just 7 years old at the time. The rest is a fogged memory. Maybe someplace in my brain refuses to remember. Doctors have diagnosed this as Dissociative amnesia. It occurs when a person blocks out **certain** information, usually associated with a stressful or **traumatic event**, making him or **her unable to remember** important personal information.

My adolescent years were going to bring destruction to my siblings and to my parents because of the poor choices I was going to make, and this was going to carry on to my adulthood. I remember the vision I had when I was three years old. I saw a man in the kitchen, throwing me up in the air. He surrounded me with peace, the type of peace I experience whenever my mom took me and my siblings to church. I remember thinking to myself, this is God. His warm smile, His everlasting love told me it was Him I saw. But that experience was short-lived. I remember the abandonment I felt as a child which I would mostly act out. I remember that when my little sister was born and my mom brought her home from the hospital, I didn't like the idea that there was another little girl there. I was ok with my brother being there, but not my sister. She was going to take my place, I thought. I remember hiding in the closet and crying. I already felt neglected, and now with her arrival, I knew I would be treated like I never existed. I wasn't the "role model type" of sibling. An older sibling can act as a positive role model when they help their younger sibling with homework or give them advice., but not me. I was jealous, difficult to get along with and started having issues with my younger ones from a very young age. Now that I look back, I wish my parents taught me the act of communication and made me feel valuable.

Teenage Life

We lived in Los Angeles, California, off the corner of Western in a small apartment building. My mother worked in a jewelry store downtown and she took the bus downtown every morning. My mother was afraid to drive, so she rode the bus everywhere she went. When I was a little girl, I remember going with my mom and my brother on the bus to run errands. My father was a branch manager for American Saving Bank at the time. They were hardly home. My parents both worked long hours, only coming home late at night to have dinner already prepared by the maid before retiring to bed afterwards. This became their routine for many years. On weekends, we did spend time together, shopping and going to lunch; but this seldom took place on Sundays after church. I started to attend Our Lady of the Holy Rosary, a school in Sun Valley, CA.

....A LITTLE BREAK... CAN I BE HONEST WITH YOU? IT IS QUITE UNCOMFORTABLE FOR ME TO GO BACK TO MY PAST, BUT I WANT TO BE SET FREE FROM THE CHAINS THAT HAVE KEPT ME LOCKED UP FOR YEARS. I NEED FREEDOM IT! GOD'S WORD SAYS "Where the Spirit of the Lord is, there is freedom, where the Spirit of the Lord is, there's no fear, where the Spirit of the Lord is, there is healing, where the Spirit of the Lord is, there is fire, where the Spirit of the Lord is, there is grace, sufficient enough." HALLELUYAH!

I attended Our Lady of Holy Rosary till 9th grade, and I didn't have that many friends. I was an outcast and I had issues with my self-esteem. Other issues started to arise with my eyes, after which my parents got me glasses. Also, I had a lazy eye. My parents took me to the doctors and I was diagnosed with an AV malformation in the brain at the age of 14. Also, I was being sexually abused by my only uncle, which I've known all my life. The same man that the family loved and admired so much, because of his strong work ethics. He could do it all, especially as it pertains to house projects. He lusted over me, and as a child, I didn't know what to do. It was sick and disgusting. I felt violated, dirty, and unclean. I was still a child. I was 14 about to be 15 years old when all of it started. From a very early age, children begin to form ideas and beliefs about themselves based on how their **parents communicate** with them. When **parents communicate** effectively with their children, they are showing them how to respect others. I had no respect for my siblings and didn't know how to communicate with my parents about my emotions and feelings. I felt abandoned, rejected, and lonely.

Late Teenage Life

It was really a tough one for me during this age gap (15 to 17). I hated my life when I was 15. I recall cutting my arms and my wrist. I didn't want to live. I hated my life, and I was starting to act out. I recall being very verbally abusive to my siblings and my parents did not know about it because they were always at work. I remember telling them "if you tell mom and dad I will hit you, and I will beat you up." They feared me and they never reported me to them. It feels so terrible trying to remember all of that right now.

I was also getting in trouble with the law, being at the wrong place at the wrong time.

Party Life

I went to jail several times because of the people I hung out with. I was constantly at the wrong place at the wrong time. The crew I was involved with was into drugs, throwing loud parties and doing other terrible vices. The saying, "show me your friend and I will tell you who you are" holds true, because my association with them resulted in various inappropriate behaviours from me. It was not long that I found myself in jail. The first time I went to jail, it was for disrupting peace. I was scared from the inside with various crazy thoughts overwhelming me. I thought to myself that if my parents found out, they would send me away or disown me. I was held behind the bars for hours after which I was given a ticket to go to court, where I was sentenced.

A few months passed after I was released and I went to a party where I was given a drink. I didn't know that this drink contained hallucination drug and right in that party, I was raped. The effects and the aftermath of the rape was a traumatic experience for me. I felt numb and isolated afterwards. The trauma of being raped or sexually assaulted can be shattering, leaving you feeling scared, ashamed, and alone or plagued by nightmares, flashbacks, and other unpleasant memories.

After school one morning, I went to my friend's house. We hung out, listened to music, and did our homework. I started to look through the contact list on her phone. She sat next to me and we started to call all the guy's numbers she had stored there. After a couple of calls, there was this particular guy who actually wanted my number. After going back and forth, I gave him my number. It wasn't long that we started talking on the phone, and we would sometimes talk for long hours every day. I felt like I finally had someone who loved me, cared about me, and was willing to listen to whatever I had to say. I lied to him about my name. I told him my name was Lisa. I told him that because I just wanted to be someone else. I hated who I was already. I felt ashamed and dirty. Lisa sounded like a pleasant name to me, so I told him it was my name. I wanted to hide my identity. For me, it sounded way better than Jennifer the crossed eyed who had no friends, been molested, controlling to her sibling, and who had a distant relationship with her parents. I didn't see him for almost a year, we just spoke on phone. I was embarrassed to see him because of my eyes. Even after I started communicating with this guy, things still remained the same at home, and my actions were neutral towards everyone. I felt numb. I just wanted to escape from everything and be in a place where I could be loved!

After countless appointments with the neurologist and my optometrist, I finally got an appointment for surgery, first on the AV malformation; then, I was going to get my eyes corrected. Finally, the shame that I felt was going to be over. No more hiding my face in school, no more lonely lunch breaks. I will finally be able to look at someone in the eye and not feel ashamed. I was 17 years old at the time when I had my surgery. I recall leaving the hospital and sitting in the front seat of my father's car and being able to look at the trees. Everything around me was one. I was not looking at the world with double vision no more. Oh what a relief and joy for me! I was able to meet my boyfriend. We hung out a lot at his home and we went to parties as all teenagers do. After the surgery, my confidence grew, and having a boyfriend by my side further gave me the assurance and the confidence to move on with my life.

On one of those days, I discovered that I missed my period. I became concerned because I didn't want to get pregnant. My dad would kill me, and my mom would be disappointed because she had spent so much money, paying for my tuition in a private school. I went to get a pregnancy test and my worst fear came to pass and alas! the test came out positive. I was literarily freaking out as I held the test result. I needed to do something about it before my parents get to know. I opted for an abortion. The thought that my Dad was going to punish me if he discovered kept racing through my mind. I went ahead with the abortion after I told my mom about it. I remember that day clearly, it was a cold day and my mom went with me. My dad picked us up at carl's junior, down the street of the abortion center. After the whole procedure, my mom and I got into the car and we were both crying. It was until a couple of minutes later that he asked what the matter was. I could hold it any longer, so I told him, I will never forget the look on his face. he was disappointment. I felt *abandoned, rejected, and lonely*

Young Mom

I felt numb, and I kept making irrational decisions based on my emotions. A couple of months later, I got pregnant again. I got a job on Ventura Blvd. working at a clothing store. During my break time at work, breaks, I would walk down the street to the bookstore and read pregnancy books. It was a good way for me to relax and it was definitely helpful for me to stay connected with my baby during this time. I didn't see much of the father because I was too busy at work and meeting new people that were

23

differently out of my league. I was learning about the blue-collar world and I really enjoyed it. I can say that I was incredibly happy during my pregnancy. When my time was due, my beautiful healthy baby boy was born and was named Joseph. The story of Joseph from the book of Genesis in the bible is one of heroic redemption and forgiveness. Joseph was the most loved son of his father, Israel, and was given the famous robe of many colors. When Joseph reported having dreams of his brothers, and even the stars and moon, bowing before him, and their jealousy and hatred of Joseph grew. His brothers sold him into slavery to a traveling caravan of the Ishmaelites who took him to Egypt and sold him to Potiphar, the captain of Pharaoh's guard.

In Egypt, the Lord's presence with Joseph enables him to find favor with Potiphar and the keeper of the prison. With God's help, Joseph interprets the dreams of two prisoners, predicting that one of them will be reinstated while the other put to death. Joseph then interprets the dreams of the Pharaoh, which anticipates seven years of plenty, followed by seven years of famine. Pharaoh recognizes Joseph's God-given ability and this prompts his promotion to the chief administrator of Egypt. I was fascinated with the story of Joseph, not only could he interpret dreams, he also had the favor with God. I still remember these stories from when I was in school. I wanted my son to have the favor that Joseph had, and to be able to interpret dreams also. It was a joyful time for me. We all connected in the family. I started being nice to my siblings. It was like this baby changed me. My parents also started spending time with me and my newborn. It was a great time, and I can say that I was extremely happy.

One day, I went to visit the father of my child. My son must have been 3 months old at the time of my visit. The thing is our relationship started to go south after my son was born. I will never forget the day I went to visit. It was Valentine's weekend and I bought balloons and chocolate, so that we could celebrate as a family. I remember waiting in the living room. When the door opened, he walked in with another woman. We exchanged some words and in the blink of an eye, my life was shattered. He left with this woman and I didn't see him again for many years. Again, I felt *abandoned, rejected, and lonely.*

Party Life

I was 19 years old at the time and I was living with my parents and siblings. I became depressed like never before. It seemed like I was walking around with a dark cloud hanging over me. I felt like every step I took would knock me to my knees. I moved out of my parent's house at the age of 21, uncertain of the future, I moved out with my friend to Sylmar and that was the beginning of my treading the path of destruction. On weekends, I would go drop off my son at his grandmother house, and I would go out with my roommate and party. I didn't start drinking till I was 25 years old, but I sure loved going out to all the nightclubs in Hollywood and in West Covina. My stay with my roommate only lasted about 2 months. Afterwards, I moved out and went back home and saved money, while living with my parents. I finally saved enough money to get my own place with my son. I now had an amazing place to stay, but my partying didn't stop. Now, not only was I drinking, I already started trying cocaine also. The only reason I tried it was because I was trying to numb and not feel all the pain. I didn't know how to face my demons, so I would drink and use them as an escape. It was as if I was in a prison with heavy chains that bound me up. These weren't even light chains; they were heavy padlocks used to lock up those chains. (ISAIAH 58:6). I was a very broken woman. I am sure you might have seen one before. She is one who has given her all and given up already. You're not exactly sure what brought her to this place of being Distant, Withdrawn, Angry, Sad, and Bitter. She is the type who has thrown in the towel and said, "two tears in a bucket, and I'm done." Externally, her hair is a mess, she is basically wasting away. When you look in her eyes, all she can do is hang her head down low. To the average eye, she is playing the victim role, she is seen as weak and it is believed that it is her fault. In this world, people could give two shits about the broken woman's story. For me, I have deposited more into others than myself. I was seeking love from lovers, friends, and family who could not give a damn about me. I didn't love me back either. When I was depleted, I had a nervous breakdown and was near death. I never knew that there is

POWER IN THE NAME OF JESUS. TO BREAK EVERY CHAIN TO BREAK EVERY CHAIN, TO BREAK EVERY CHAIN.

It was the aha moment for me. I knew something had to change, I slowed down. It wasn't long afterwards that, I got into a relationship with an older man

New Man

The new guy I got into a relationship with happens to come from El Salvador. He was born and raised there. There is a sharp contrast between the American traditional values and theirs. For example, in El Salvador, men are taught to be the one to provide for the needs of the family, while their wives stay at home with the kids. That doesn't happen here in America. In fact, in America, women need to work in order to survive and live comfortably. I eventually had two children for him as the course of our relationship progressed. I thought I had met my ideal man already. I tried to move things forward WAY too quickly, usually, because I was needy and was seeking out emotional validation to make me feel whole, something I don't feel on my own. He was like no man I have ever dated. He happens to be the complete opposite of me. I am fire and he is water. He likes to stay in his comfort zone, while I on the other hand loved to explore places. In the beginning of our relationship, I didn't know how to communicate at all. I didn't understand the ways he communicates. due to his calm nature. Due to the communication gap, my past started creeping up again. I started going out with my friends to parties and clubs, which eventually led to me cheating on my boyfriend. We were not married; he was just the father of my kids. It wasn't long after this that I ended things with him. At this time, my life was becoming a total mess already. My siblings didn't want to be around me, because whenever I came to visit for the holidays, or they came by to see me, I was either drunk or drinking. I was so ashamed of my life and I found solace in drinking, instead of turning back to God.

I choose to live without Christ. There were times I could come to him and surrender and have him lead him. But I compared God with my earthly father. Can I have a relationship with God despite how I have messed up? I thought to myself, GOD will *abandon* me eventually and I will feel *alone* and *rejected* again.

I grew up in a dysfunctional home and it had a negative effect on my behavior and feelings as an adult. I was one of those negative people with a negative mindset who kept thinking nothing good was going to come out of her life or future. The trauma of the molestation further took a toll in my life, thus causing me to develop essential yet **unhealthy survival habits.**

I also learned how to live with "dysfunction as normal" since I was not used to a life without chaos. To gain freedom from my past, I needed to learn exactly how this had impacted me, but without Jesus in my life, I was stuck like a parked car going nowhere. A prisoner in my own mind, I started to realize where I was. I don't know how I got here, but I became aware I was in a prison in my mind. The anxiety, and depression I was carrying on my shoulders were unbearable. I was a broken woman.

The Affair

I was a stay at home mom who worked at nights and stayed home during the day. The distance between myself and the father of my kids grew and eventually, I fell in love with someone else. I ended up marrying this man and we moved to Nevada together to start a family. He was different from the father of my children. He enjoyed golfing and we would sometimes go to the golf course while also traveling with the kids. He enjoyed fishing and he taught my kids fishing. This was a different lifestyle than the one I had been exposed to. He did enjoy a tall can of beer every other day. I would sometimes join him and there were times we would get drunk and fight afterwards. I wanted to stop, but I couldn't. I was basically raised in the church, but here I am, I have been in and out of church all of my life. I wanted to serve the Lord, but I didn't know how. My desire for drinking was greater for my desire for God. I had no self-control.

My husband ended up getting a promotion from his job and the promotion was going to move him to another state, Las Vegas. We ended up moving there with my children, where he bought me a house

There was a church close by to where we lived, and I seriously wanted to go. In as much I wanted to retrace my steps and go back to God, I also didn't want to mess up this perfect relationship. I was in a fix.

Life in Vegas
Finding Christ

I wanted my life to be different and it was, but the only thing that was missing to make it compete was my older son who decided to stay in California. I drove to California frequently to see my parents and my older son. I started to attend the beautiful Pentecostal church close to my house in Las Vegas. This time around, I got involved right away. I got baptized and that was where my **transformation** began without my knowledge. I enjoyed Sunday services so much that I would usually stay for the second service. At every service I attended, it was as if the Pastor was speaking to me about my hurt and my pain. I started to feel a sense of peace and love. That same type of peace which I experienced when I was three years old. It's the peace that passes all understanding. It doesn't make sense to the world, but this peace is very real and available for everyone to experience.

Once I was able to understand **John 10:10 which says** *"the thief comes only to kill, steal, and destroy, but I have come that they may have life and life more abundantly."* I didn't know that the devil hated everyone in the world, and wanted nothing but destruction in my family. I knew he was the enemy, but I didn't understand how much hatred he had toward God's children.

I surrendered my life to Christ, laid it at the altar and I was ready to take that next step of healing and restoration. I knew it wasn't going to be easy, but I was ready to go on this journey with God and trust the process. As time went on, my commitment to the church grew and I started to grow apart from my husband. He started to go to places that I had no desire to go to. This led us to having many discussions as regards my new found faith.

One night, while in my children's room, crying, I heard the voice of God tell me that he loved me. The scripture God laid in my heart was *"my sheep know my voice and another they will not follow."* I fell asleep like a baby that night. I woke up the next morning thinking about everything that has been happening again. I knew deep down inside that my place was in Los Angeles, but a part of me didn't want to go. I started feeling deep down in me that if I didn't go back home, something bad would happen, I just had a bad unceasing feeling. The truth of the matter is that I was supposed to have left a long time ago, but I still was trying to control everything. I didn't want to go, and God was not going to let me stay when He knew my destiny was somewhere else.

This is what surrendering to God's will looks like. Even though you don't understand or have it all figured out, you just have to trust him. This whole trust thing had me confused. The more I continued in studying the word and praying, then more He started to lead me on an amazing journey of recovery and that was what I really needed. I was just so broken that I knew it was going to be an overnight transformation, it was going to be a process.

(Psalms 147:3 He heals the brokenhearted and binds up their wounds (healing their pain and comforting their sorrow)

I knew it was going to be little by little, step by step, precept upon precept, line upon line, just like a baby who is learning to walk and I was ready to pay the price.

As I continued in my walk with Jesus, more light started showing on my path, even though it wasn't easy. One day, I packed all of my belongings and left Las Vegas and never went back again. This time, it was different. I left with peace and understanding that everything was going to be ok, the transformation within me was taking place. For the first time, I didn't feel *alone, abandoned, and rejected.*

BABY STEPS

After I left Las Vegas, I returned back to my mother's house with my children. I started looking back at my life and how God protected me from harm and danger. While I was out there in the streets, free as a bird, drinking at times and even driving home drunk, something bad could have happened to me or to another person. I fought the battle of my drinking habit for 20 years. I did so much damage, and have hurt a lot of people, especially the father of my children. It took something drastic in my life to listen to what God was trying to tell me.

I was grateful to God that I was back home with all my children. I have come to appreciate each day. Each day is a gift from God. The Bible says in **Proverbs 27:1, _"Do not boast about tomorrow, for you do not know what a day may bring."_** In other words, tomorrow is not promised to any of us. I couldn't do anything about the past, but I know I have the power to change my future. It starts off by thinking positive, by telling yourself that something good is going to happen to me today. I started the day off right by thinking positive thoughts, something I had never tried before. I was used to saying negative things about myself, my family, and my circumstances. Now, based on the new programming of my mind, what I was doing was prophesying my future *(Proverbs 23:7 For as he thinks in his heart so is, he)*. I now had to pay attention to whatever word was coming out of my mouth; was I prophesying great things into my future or was I saying otherwise? I decided to speak words of life into my future, and not curse it anymore. I started on a positive note. One thing I came to realize was that, God can bring beauty from the ashes of our lives. The next morning, I got up and went to church. That same week, I started volunteering at a school. This school was a special school,

39

meaning that it specialized in working with kids with special needs. From my past experiences, I knew in my heart that I wanted to help people by providing care and support and helping them become more independent and confident in their own abilities and making a difference. I volunteered at the school for 6 months before attending Los Angeles Valley College.

College Life

As soon as I started school, I became scared. I had all of these painful, negative thoughts because of my past experience in high school, especially how I was made fun of and teased. I wasn't an "A" student and I had difficulty learning. All of these emotions and feelings started to make me anxious, but nonetheless, I gave it a shot. I kept an index card with bible verses around the house. I remembered one in particular. It was the index card in front of the mirror in my bathroom and written on it was my favorite verse: *Jeremiah 29:11- For I know the plans I have for you,"* *declares the LORD, "plans to prosper you and not to harm* *you, plans to give you hope and a future.* I took a class in child development and got an A. I remember crying and feeling a sense of accomplishment. I decided to enroll full time and maintained a high GPA. It wasn't easy for me, so to keep up, I made sure I enrolled myself in support groups. For instance, I enrolled in the TRiO program. The TRiO Program is a support system designed for first-generation, low income, and/or disabled students. TRiO is not an acronym. The Federal TRIO Programs (TRIO, also stylized as TRiO) are federal outreach and student services programs in the United States designed to identify and provide services for individuals from disadvantaged backgrounds. They are administered, funded, and implemented by the United States Department of Education. TRIO includes eight programs targeted to serve and assist low-income individuals, first-generation college students, and individuals with disabilities to progress through the academic pipeline from middle school to post-baccalaureate programs. The support system consists of individual counseling, individual tutoring, academic workshops, cultural activities, transfer information, computer labs, and complimentary school supplies. All of these services are provided free of charge and exclusively to TRiO students. I was at the Trio office every day, staying on course. I needed all the help I could get and, also, it was free.

One evening, my oldest son called me to let me know that I was going to be a grandmother. As I was driving to the hospital, I remember asking God to please perform a miracle. My oldest son was going to name my grandson Manson. All that came to my mind was Charles Manson. That's crazy I thought I asked God to please touch my son's heart and give him a name from the Bible. God did answer my prayers. My grandson was born, and christened Noah, Isaiah (*Mathew 7:7 Ask, and you shall receive*). The Lord gave my grandson two powerful leaders' names, and one of them happened to be a prophet. Hallelujah! (*Psalm 37 :4 Delight yourself in the LORD, and he will give you the desires of your heart*).

Married Life

I eventually went back to the father of my children and we got married in 2014. We have had our ups and downs like every other couple, but this time, it was different. I was more focused on my future and I let go of my past by asking God to help me Turn my Test into a Testimony and turn the evil the enemy had for me around (*Job 1:7 And though your beginning was small, your latter days will be very great*). One evening as I was driving back from my cousin's house,

I was pulled over by the cops because of expired tags. The police officer gave me a court date. I went to court and instead of me paying the ticket, I was asked to go do time in jail. I was afraid and I didn't want to go back behind those cold bars. The Bible verse that readily came to my mind was Psalm 32:7, *I cried out to the Lord, and he answered me. He delivered me from all my fears*. I did the time in jail and I recall expressing my love to the inmates and sharing God's word with them. I could hear God say to me from the first time I set my foot there, "welcome to your ministry." (*Isaiah 61:1 The spirit of the Lord is upon me because the Lord hath anointed me to preach good tidings to the poor; He has sent me to heal the brokenhearted, to proclaim liberty to the captives, and the opening of the prison for those who are bound*). I became more surrendered to his will and his purpose for my life. I knew that his blueprint was much greater than mine. When I got out, I struggled with God to do what was right. During this time, God was restoring my relationship with my parents and I was still struggling with an unforgiving spirit. It was a bit difficult to let go of the physical, verbal, and emotional pain that I was carrying. In the end, God did restore me. God can restore what has been lost and broken. (*Ephesians 4:32 Be kind and compassionate to one another, forgiving each other, just as in Christ God forgave you*).

A Father's Love

My relationship with my father was a distant one, more distant than that of my mother. My father had been given a flu shot back in 2000 and as a result, he ended up becoming extremely ill and became paralyzed from his neck down. As a family, we decided to place him in a rehabilitation home where he received 24-hour care and he lived there for 16 years. I usually go to visit my father at any slightest opportunity I had. In the beginning, it was quite difficult. He was so controlling and verbally abusive, and he can be hurtful with his words to everyone around him. As time went on, I became aware that this was not easy for him as well. Right from the time I got know him, he had been an independent man, and also a very opinionated and sometimes rash person who doesn't hesitate to show it, both at home and in public. He was so used to doing everything on his own and his way. Now knowing that he had to depend on nurses and family was going to be his biggest challenge ever.

(Exodus 20:12 Honor your father and mother. Then you will live a long, full life in the land the LORD your God is giving you).

How can I improve my relationship with my father when I feel he is somewhat of a stranger to me? Well, I started by listening to him. This was extremely challenging for me. Because he didn't talk, he mostly yelled and screamed and felt frustrated. I had to be honest and let my father know the things that bothered me and the areas that needed improvement as it pertains to our relationship. I had to learn to be quick to forgive and ask for my father's forgiveness. I had to learn to be humble, stay quiet, and trust God in the process. Our relationship started to blossom, even though it took time. I could see his attitude towards me change, little by little. He became loving, gentle, and considerate. He started to open up to me about his life. We started to have deep and meaningful conversations. On a couple of occasions, he would tell me he was proud of me, and just hearing those words was like music to my ears. Mostly after our conversations, I would leave the hospital inspired and happy. I felt connected and complete. All my life, I felt something was missing. I guess that missing piece was me not having an open relationship with my parents. I finally had it, especially with my father. I was complete. As the years passed, and he started ageing, his strength began to drop, it wasn't like it was anymore; his words of encouragement were there, and his faith in God was strong. But I could see him depleting slowly. On October 30, 2016, my father went home to be with the Lord. He fought during the last 16 years of his life, and now, he has finished his course. It is hard to put how it feels into words when you lose your either of your parents. Everyone grieves differently. I felt peace and sadness at the same time. Peace, because I knew he had gone to a better place and sadness because I was never going to see him again. I didn't think it was going to affect me so **profoundly**, but it did. What I learned is that the death of a loved one can transform a person for the better or for worse. The man that was giving me hope and cheering me on was gone. I didn't have anyone to believe in me anymore. But I wasn't alone, God comforted me during this tough time

Backslidden

Psalms 34:18 The Lord is close to the brokenhearted and saves those who are crushed in the spirit.

I felt broken once again. I still continued with school and work, but I was still carrying a heavy burden. All of a sudden, I fell into the enemy's trap of using alcohol to self-medicate and to avoid the pain. I started becoming a functioning alcoholic again.

I became frustrated with my weakness; it was like a thorn in my flesh. I went back to the madness and the craziness that alcohol and substance abuse causes. I went back to that pit of hell that God rescued me from. I went back to what was comfortable because sometimes we look at the dysfunction as normal behavior. I was getting rid of my pain and my trauma by practicing more destructive behaviors because this is what alcohol and substance abuse does and it causes me to act crazy. When you're under the influence you feel like everyone is against you, but that is not usually the case. For me, my actions were causing the people around me to withdraw, and they were looking at me like I was never going to change. Also I didn't realize that the people around me might feel scared and nervous because of my behavior and my emotions being up and down.

That is what alcohol does to me, it causes me to start tripping out, who wants to be around someone that can't even function. I felt ashamed and guilty. I developed my own system of survival, but during that whole time, God never left me, and I know He will never leave you too (*Hebrews 13:5, I will never leave you nor forsake you*).

God rescued me again from a dangerous and destroying situation. Again, I wanted to get better because I have seen and experienced how much of transformation can do in a life. God loves us so much that He doesn't want to leave us broken and miserable. He wants to see us set free and delivered.

I remember asking God for forgiveness and telling Him that I had repented of my sins as I grabbed my bible and the Lord whispered in my ear to read the story of the prodigal son. The parable of the prodigal son indicates, however, that we do have the opportunity to make a change; we do not have to stay in our hopeless state; we can come to ourselves. The lost son realized that in his father's house there was sustenance for him; he humbled himself, willing, if necessary, to be his father's servant, and went back home. This turning in our lives is the first indication of God's love for us. Even recognizing our sinful, hopeless state is initiated in us by God, Himself. (*Romans 2:4; Or do you show contempt for the riches of his kindness, tolerance, and patience, not realizing that God's kindness leads you toward repentance*).

I didn't restitute with God because I was scared. I looked at God as my earthly parents. I felt God was mad at me and embarrassed, because of my rebellion and stubborn ways, always wanting to do it my way and wouldn't want to take me back. I was having trouble trusting God. My earthly father was gone and for the longest time, I was walking around with a grieving spirit. How many times do we walk around with a grieving heart, listening to the lies of the enemy?

The devil kept telling me I was the black sheep, the bad apple, the odd duck, the black swan, the ugly duckling, a nobody God and that was never going to use me. The devil kept telling me I had no purpose or Divine Destiny. He kept telling me I WAS NEVER GOING TO CHANGE. All of these thoughts were rapidly coming to my mind. The enemy started to convince me that I should just END IT ALL.

Bounce back

All of a sudden, a sense of peace overtook my mind and body.

(*2 Timothy 1:7 For God has not given us a spirit of fear, but of power and of love and of a sound mind*)

That day, the Lord said to me, "Arise, continue on the path, I have set before you." (*Psalm 118:24, This is the day that the Lord has made; Let us rejoice and be glad in it*). It was surprising that I could still remember that scripture.

I looked at the sentence and meditated. In a loud voice, I declared, "I command my day. I have **victory** over today and my life. My day will prosper." I started speaking words of life throughout my day. I started declaring "my day is going to be a good day, full of God's love and favor. Favor follows me everywhere throughout the day. I rejoice. I am happy. I am glad for another day of life, health, and prosperity."

I started to develop habits of peace, rest, and hope. My life started to make more sense when I started speaking life and life more abundantly. Yes, there were times I felt discouraged because things were all out of order at home, work, and school. There were times I woke up upset and angry about what I was going through, but do I because of that command my day to fall apart? I needed to change my negative thought pattern because the truth of the matter is that it wouldn't get me anywhere and I will ultimately stay stuck like a parked car not going anywhere.

I still continued to speak life and started to thank God, believing that my situation was going to change. Instead of murmuring and complaining, I just went into praise. I am created in God's perfect image. I have the DNA of a winner. Favor follows me throughout the day. I am the head and not the tail, above and not beneath. I have a divine destiny ahead of me. I am God's perfect blueprint. It doesn't matter where

I start, all that matters is where I finish. All the possibilities and endless opportunities are in front of me, bouncing back big in is my goal.

Even though I went back to my old ways, but I learned from it. I got up, dusted myself off, and continued my race and stayed on track (*Philippians 1:6, being confident of this, that he who began a good work in you will carry it on to completion until the day of Christ Jesus*).

Thank God, for the healing process, this is where you let the chips fall where they may. Let God do what He does best, that is, fighting your battles (*Deuteronomy 3:22 You shall not fear them, for it is the Lord your God who fights for you*).

This is the beginning of a process, there is still so much to do, but don't worry about tomorrow (*Matthew 6:34, Therefore do not worry about tomorrow, for tomorrow will worry about itself)*. Worry does not empty tomorrow of its troubles, what it does it empties your strength for today. There were times that I woke up and felt distracted, discouraged, and unqualified, but whenever I picked up my bible and I read about all the people God used, I discover each time that they were mostly regular people. I usually tell myself afterwards that I am qualified. God is willing to use anyone, even with their imperfections.

Abraham was old

David committed adultery

Jacob was a liar

Noah was a drunk

Isaac was a daydreamer

Leah was ugly

Samson had long hair and was a womanizer

John was self-righteous

Naomi was bitter

Miriam was a gossiper

Moses was a murderer

Solomon was a polygamist

Matthew was a tax collector

Rahab was a prostitute

Jeremiah was to young

Gideon was afraid

Elijah was suicidal

Jonah ran from God

Isaiah preached naked

You don't have to be perfect. In fact, we will never be. Just be willing to be used and see what God has in store for you.

WHAT AM I DOING NOW?

When no one encouraged me, I encouraged myself. Staying in the church keep me grounded and safe. Going to church means you become part of the parish family. It's not something you do by yourself, it's a reminder that you are not alone. You do this together, with other people, which will remind you that you have a supportive community by your side. These community members may become some of your closest friends. The people you see every Sunday will look for you to say hello. They will miss you if you aren't there. They will keep you in their thoughts in prayers in a time of need. They will encourage and support you (*Psalms:100 2and3, Serve the Lord with gladness! Come into his presence with singing! Know that the Lord is God!*

It is he who made us, and we are his; we are his people and the sheep of his pasture).

I started to attend AA meetings and I stayed connected with organizations that were helping me move forward. I also attended therapy. **Therapy** helped me control my emotions whenever problems came or I felt stressed, even if they aren't dramatically life-altering or traumatic. **Therapy** is well-known for its problem-solving techniques and reputation **as** a tool for overcoming anxiety, depression, and addiction. But for me, it was overcoming these three monkeys that would crawl up my back from time to time. It was about was me feeling *alone, abandoned, and rejected*.

It felt good to talk about my emotions and feelings. It helped me to create a blueprint to focus on the next day. I keep my blueprint simple: God first and community help secondly (therapy, church, etc.). Continuing on seeking counseling professionally and receiving counseling at school was also helping me make better choices. This resulted is better communication with my husband and kids. You have to know how to respond when there is a heated argument at home. What I discovered was not to say anything at all that was negative, and to respond in a calm matter. But most of the time, I turned the other cheek, not saying anything at all. This was the first step of personal growth. This principle was extremely difficult for me. It took some time and it didn't happen overnight. I talked to God about it. Sometimes, God will fight the actual battle through you, other times He will simply tell you to hold your peace and do absolutely nothing, and then He will move Himself to completely take out the attack coming against you. This is where God shows you how powerful and awesome He really is when He moves into battle to personally protect you.

You have to stay still. This is also a process that you eventually master. God wants to see you happy by seeking him first and helping yourself by staying in therapy. These two simple keys will help you on your journey to recover. The journey of a thousand miles begins with one step (*Isaiah 54:17, No weapon that is formed against thee shall prosper; and every tongue that shall rise against thee in judgment thou shalt condemn. This is the heritage of the servants of the LORD, and their righteousness is of me, saith the LORD*).

FINAL THOUGHT

Don't lose your vision, you were created for a time as this. Your assignment, no one else can fulfill but you. I know the saying is work on your strengths, not your weakness, but I worked on my weakness, I was not going to let my weakness take me down anymore. Where I am weak, God is strong. I am fighting the good fight of faith. When God has an encounter with you, you experience a radical transformation. The first step to this amazing transformation is to forgive yourself. Too many of us don't forgive ourselves and we walk around bruised and broken. This starts the healing process. You must forgive yourself and those who hurt you. This process is not easy and it's going to take time, but please be patient with this process. It might be short, and it might belong, but you will experience joy and peace in your heart. Ask the Lord to reveal your childhood pain. The pain that you experience by being rejected and left alone. God loves us so much he doesn't want to see us broken and miserable; He wants to see us set free and delivered

God can turn your scares into stars

God can give you beauty for ashes

God can turn your test into a testimony

Is there anything too hard for the Lord? No, not one? The right decisions you make will also help you move forward and stay on track. We all face huge mountains in our lives, but don't let the mountain define who you are, you have to have a mountain-moving faith. That mountain of drugs, that mountain of alcohol, that mountain of depression, that mountain of loneliness, that mountain of fear, speak to those mountains that has you chained up, it's time to cast it down. You have to speak to your mountain. Jesus said in **Mark 11:23** "For verily I say unto you, that whosoever shall say unto this mountain, be thou removed, and be thou cast into the sea; and shall not doubt in his heart, but shall believe that those things which he saith shall come to pass; he shall have whatsoever he saith.

I have learned throughout the years that if you do not speak to your mountain your mountain will speak to you. You must believe that the mountain will come crumbling down once you speak to it. It's time to get yourself moving and passionately get on with your life and the purpose which God has created for.

Conclusion

I pray a blessing over you what the Devil meant for evil, God will turn it around for your good. God will restore the years that the canker worm and the locust have eaten (Joel 2:25) and will give you double for your trouble (Isaiah 61).

May the God of hope fill you with all the joy and peace as you trust in him, so that you may overflow with hope by the power of the holy spirit.

If God did it for me, He can do it for you. You have not been buried you have been planted.

Your best days are ahead of you!

YOUR BLUEPRINT

This guide will walk you through the steps.

1) SAFE HAVEN

Find a clean and safe environment where you can see yourself progressing and moving forward. Having a safe haven (a safe place to live) will help you move forward in life. This doesn't mean you have to stay at your family home if this is where you have unresolved problems. It can be at a friend's house that you trust or at a halfway house.

2) SUPPORT GROUP

Enrolling in a rehabilitation program its extremely important. It will help you and may even save your relationship with your family. Family is the single most important influence in a child's life. From their first moments of life, children depend on parents and family to protect them and provide for their needs. They are a child's first teachers and act as role models in how to act and how to experience the world around them.

Deal with the problem head on. If you're an addict or an alcoholic, there's something going on mentally and emotionally that keeps you returning to these substances, even in the face of negative consequences. To that end, rehab isn't about the substances themselves; it's about discovering and addressing the reasons you keep going back to them- time and time again- even though you know they're destroying your life. Perhaps there's unresolved trauma from your childhood. Maybe the death of a loved one has left you in a semi-permanent state of depression. Maybe there are undiagnosed psychiatric issues that are driving you to subconsciously self-medicate. Joining a support group and going to counseling will help you identify the root cause of your addiction cycle.

3) SPIRITUAL ENCOUNTER

Build a relationship with God! Often, we compare God with our earthly father, which is far from the truth of who God is. GOD is a Father who is loving, caring, and gentle. He is patient and loves you so much He gave His only Son as a sacrifice for you!

John 3:16 "For God so loved the world that he gave his one and only Son, that whoever believes in him shall not perish but have eternal life."

Trust the process. You are the main priority in your recovery. It is when you finally let go and commit to the process of your journey to recovery that the gleaning of wisdom will turn into much knowledge and self-awareness. Joy and relief come from finally seeing that there is hope, and that there is actually a life waiting for you that can be free from the shackles of addiction. And finally, the structure of a life well-lived-- where you are bettering yourself and learning about yourself, and repairing relationships--is much more enticing than the chaos and narrowness of a life rooted in an addiction that robbed you of everything beautiful and everything that matters in your life.

Always remember: you are the main focal point in the process of recovery!

Here is what to do, if you can't go home, or don't have a safe place to go to.

Project Roomkey

Project Roomkey is a collaborative effort by the State, County, and the Los Angeles Homeless Services Authority (LAHSA) to secure hotel and motel rooms for vulnerable people experiencing homelessness. Project Roomkey aims to not only protect high-risk individuals, but to also prevent the spread of the deadly virus in our communities and protect the capacity of our hospitals and healthcare system.

Apply for Housing or Section 8

Apply for transitional housing

Apply and call your homeless shelters

Here is what to do if you can't afford therapy. The NAMI Help Line can help you with anything- other than a crisis situation- under the mental health umbrella. They can answer questions like, "Where's the closest free support group near me?" or "How do I find low-cost treatment?" Call them at 1-800-950-NAMI (6264) or email them at info@nami.org.

Look up information in the Substance Abuse and Mental Health Services Administration (SAMHA) treatment Locator. This is a comprehensive national organization that can locate low-cost therapy options, support groups, and free mental health clinics. Find a therapist who has a sliding scale that can reduce the cost of therapy based on your situation. Based on how much you make, you might be able to get up to 50% to 70% off. They will ask you how much you think you can pay and how much you make. Most therapists take on a number of clients for free so ask if they have any "pro bono" spots open. Keep in mind that every licensed clinician out there has an ethics code that they adhere to and part of that ethics code says that they're supposed to provide some of our services free of charge as a gesture of "goodwill." Ask and you may receive!

People training to be psychologists, social workers, and family therapists have to get on-the-job experience. Find a counseling office or college with a counseling department that may offer their counseling or therapy services that will be heavily discounted or even free. Don't worry about seeing a trainee, they will also be supervised by someone who's licensed.

If you are a student, take advantage of the free campus resources. Look into support groups or therapy groups which are cheaper or free

Pastoral counseling —get counseling from a trained minister, rabbi, priest, imam, etc. — it is usually free and another thing to look into.

This section was derived from the following links:

https://www.shadowmountainrecovery.com/blog/25/trusting-the-process

https://www.inc.com/amy-morin/5-ways-mentally-strong-people-deal-with-rejection.html

https://www.verywellmind.com/loneliness-causes-effects-and-treatments-2795749

A Deeper Look

The Blueprint is extremely important to a way of recovery. It will help you break an emotional addiction with the effects of *rejection*. Most likely, you have been dealing with the effects of rejection as a child and grew up feeling rejected all your life. Preparing yourself to be mentally strong is part of the journey you are taking. Mentally strong people know that rejection serves as proof that they're living life to the fullest. They expect to be rejected sometimes, and they're not afraid to go for "it", even when they suspect it may be a long shot. If you never get rejected, you may be living too far inside your comfort zone. You can't be sure you're pushing yourself to your limits until you get turned down every now and then. When you get rejected for a project, passed up for a job, or turned down by a friend, you'll know you're putting yourself out there.

The Effects of Abandonment

I have felt the effects of **abandonment** from the time. When I was born, both of my parents worked, and I was raised by a housekeeper and babysitter. This feeling sucks. Dealing with abandonment in your group program and therapy will help you move past these issues, because you will be surrounded by people who care and want to see you further yourself in your career and in life.

The Effects of Loneliness

Loneliness is very detrimental to a person's life, and it can lead to death. It has a wide range of negative effects on both physical and mental health that includes depression and suicide. It can cause people to feel empty, alone, and unwanted. This is absolutely the worst feeling ever. That's why it is important to face these situations and not run from them anymore. I have provided a list of resources where you can seek help. Remember, you are the main priority. You need to stay stable and grounded before moving forward in your life. Locating a support group and seeking counseling will help you stay grounded. Reading your Bible-the word of God- will help you remember God's promises to you as you recover from a past journey into a new person in Christ. Be patient! This is not going to happen overnight. It will take time, and you will heal little by little.

Here is where the healing process starts:

"Be strong and courageous. Do not be afraid or terrified because of them, for the LORD your God goes with you; he will never leave you or forsake you" (Deuteronomy 31:6).

Resources

Emergency food resource

What Are Food Banks?

Food Banks are distribution hubs. They supply the food to the Soup Kitchens, Food Pantries, Shelters, etc. They in turn provide that food to the individuals that need it. Food Banks do not directly serve individuals in need.

Homeless Shelter Directory.org

This website will help you locate the nearest food bank or soup kitchen in your area. Just click the state you are in, and the location and it will take you to the nearest place to receive food.

Office of Justice Programs (U.S. Department of Justice)

www.justice.gov/archive/fbci/progmenu_reentry.html

NationalHomeless.org

This is a national network of people who are currently experiencing or who have experienced homelessness, activists and advocates, community-based and faith-based service providers, and others committed to a single mission: To end and prevent homelessness while ensuring the immediate needs of those experiencing homelessness are met and their civil rights are respected and protected.

The Food and Nutrition Service (FNS)

www.fns.usda.gov/programs

FoodOnFoot.org

Food on Foot is a nonprofit dedicated to assisting our homeless and low-income neighbors in Los Angeles with nutritious meals, clothing, and a fresh start through a life-skills education, full-time employment, and permanent housing.

MidnightMission.org

The Midnight Mission offers a way to self-sufficiency for men, women and children that are experiencing homelessness in Los Angeles.

Unitedwayla.org

The United Way L.A. seeks to create pathways out of poverty for all L.A. County residents through education, housing, and workforce development (job placement).

Prayers you can use

I have a list of prayers to command your morning, that will start you off on a journey of faith and triumph in Christ Jesus. These prayers will help set the tone for your day. Speak it out loud every morning

PRAYERS TO COMMAND THE MORNING

- Father, God, in the name of Jesus I declare Your Lordship over this day.

- I get under Your covering and anointing of the early riser.

- I command the morning to take hold of the ends of the earth and shake the wicked out of it (Job 38:12)

- I will have dominion over the devil in the morning (Ps. 49:14).

- Lord, make me to rejoice in the outgoings of the morning (Ps. 65:8).

- I receive Your lovingkindness every morning (Ps. 143:8).

- Release the beauty of Your holiness from the womb of the morning (Ps. 110:3).

- Let Your light break forth in my life as the morning (Ps. 58:8).

- Let Your judgments come upon the enemy morning by morning) Isa 28:19).

- Lord, my going forth is prepared as the morning, and I pray that You will come as the rain, the latter and the former rain upon the earth. (Hos. 6:3).

- Lord, You will visit me every morning (Job 7:18).

- Lord, you will awaken me morning by morning. You waken my ear to hear as the learned (Isa 50:4).

- I will not be afraid of the arrow that flies by day or the terror that comes at night (Ps 91:5).

- Lord, show forth Your salvation in my life from day to day (Ps. 96:2).

- Lord, release mysteries to me to bring heaven down to earth.

- I come into agreement with the heavens to declare Your Glory.

- The chief Angels with their flaming swords are fighting on my behalf ahead of time.

- My appointed times have been declared by God in the heavens.
- At sunrise, the dawn will give birth to the will of God and light will shine upon the wickedness to shake it from the heavens.
- At twilight my enemies shall flee and newly founded spoils will await me at my destination.
- My destiny is inevitable.
- O God, let my prayers reach You this morning.
- I command the morning, its' ears to open to me and hear my cry.

- I command the earth to get in place to receive heavenly instructions on my behalf.
- I command all the elements of creation to heed and obey.

- As my praise resounds and the day breaks, the earth shall yield her increase unto me.

- I declare the first light has come.

- The first fruit of my morning is holy and the entire day is holy.

- I prophesy the will of God to the morning so the dayspring dawn will know its place in my day.

- I declare that the first light will shake the wickedness from the four corners of the earth.

- The lines, my portion are fallen on my behalf in pleasant, sweet, agreeable places and I have a secure heritage.

- I am strategically lined up with the ladder that touches the third heaven and sits on the earth. The Angels are descending and ascending according to the words I speak. Whatever is bound or loose on earth is already bound or loose in heaven.

- Revelation, healing, deliverance, salvations, peace, joy, relationships, finances, promotions...... and resources that have been demonically blocked are being loosed unto me, NOW!

- I am contagiously blessed!

- As I command the morning and capture the day, time is being redeemed.

- The people of God have taken authority over the fourth watch of the day.

- The spiritual airways and highways are being hi-jacked for Jesus.

- The atmosphere of the airways over me, my family, my Church, workplace, ministry, neighborhood, city, nation, and the world is producing a new climate. This new climate is constructing a Godly stronghold in times of trouble.

- The thinking of people will be conducive to the agenda of the Kingdom of Heaven.

- Every demonic agenda, evil thought pattern designed against the agenda of the Kingdom of Heaven is destroyed at the root of conception in Jesus' Name.

- No longer will we accept just anything and everything that is dealt to us in our days, we take our place by force.

- We declare that the Kingdom of God has come and the will of God be done on earth as it is in Heaven.

- As the sun rises, let it shine favorably upon the people of God.

- Daily, destiny is my portion because I have no thought for tomorrow.
- I am riding on the wings of the morning into a new day of victory.
- The Lord has given me dominion over all the elements and the works of His Hands.
- He has placed them under my feet because I fear the Name of the Lord. The Son of righteousness shall arise with healing in His wings and I shall tread down the wicked until they become ashes under my feet.

- I begin to walk in this dominion daily.
- I decree and declare a new day, a new season, and a fresh anointing.
- The ingredients of my destiny are programmed into my days, years, and seasons.

- I bind every evil force that try to capture my destiny, in Jesus Name.

- I plea the Blood of Jesus over every principality, power, and ruler of darkness and spiritual wickedness in high places assigned against the purposes of God for my life, my family and my Church, my city, my nation.

- I bind every destiny thief; I bind every destiny pirate and destiny devourer in the Name of Jesus. They are dethroned and dismantled in Jesus' Name. I declare they have no influence over my days.

- Every curse sent against my day is bound and broken and rendered powerless and sent to the Cross.

  I displace the luciferian spirit; I bind every false light bearer in Jesus Name. My prayers will disrupt dark plans and give my enemies a non-prosperous day.

- I have victory over my enemies
- My day will prosper.
- This is the day that the Lord has made and I will rejoice and be exceedingly glad in it!

Scripture References

John 10:10 The thief comes only to kill, steal, and destroy, but I have come that they may have life and life more abundantly.

Proverbs 6:31 If he is caught (The Thief) he must pay seven folds.

Deuteronomy 3:22 Don't not be afraid of them, the Lord your God himself will fight for you.

Psalms 118 :24 This is the day the Lord has made I will rejoice and be glad in it.

Psalms 147:3 He heals the brokenhearted and binds up their wounds (healing their pain and comforting their sorrow)

Proverbs 27:1 Do not boast, brag about tomorrow, each day brings its own surprise.

Proverbs 23:7 For as a man thinks in his heart so is he

Jeremiah 29:11 For I know the plans I have for you," declares the LORD, "plans to prosper you and not to harm you, plans to give you hope and a future.

Mathew 7:7 Ask and you shall receive

Psalm 37:4 Delight yourself in the LORD, and he will give you the desires of the heart

Job 1:7 And though your beginning was small, your latter days will be very great

Psalms 32:7 I cried out to the Lord, and he answered me;

He delivered me from all my fears,

Ephesians 4:32 Be kind and compassionate to one another, forgiving each other, just as in Christ God forgave you.

Exodus 20:12 Honor your mother and your father so you can live a long life

Psalms 34:18 The Lord is close to the brokenhearted and saves those who are crushed in the spirit.

Hebrews 13:5 I will never leave you nor forsake you

2 Timothy 1:7 For God has not given us a spirit of fear but of LOVE, POWER, and a sound Mind

Romans 2:4 It's God's kindness that leads us to repentance

Philippians 1:6 Be confident of this very thing that he who has begun a good work will complete until the day of Jesus.

Deuteronomy 3:22 Don't not be afraid of them, the Lord your God himself will fight for you.

Matthew 6:34 Therefore do not worry about tomorrow for tomorrow will worry about itself each day has enough trouble of its own

Psalm 100: 2 -3 Serve the Lord with gladness! Come into his presence with singing! Know that the Lord is God! It is he who made us, and we are his; we are his people and the sheep of his pasture.

Mark 11:23 For verily I say unto you, That whosoever shall say unto this mountain, Be thou removed, and be thou cast into the sea; and shall not doubt in his heart, but shall believe that those things which he saith shall come to pass; he shall have whatsoever he saith.

Joel 2:25 I will restore to you the years that the locust has eaten the cankerworm and the caterpillar and the palmerworm. My great army I will send among you

Ephesians 3:20- Now to him who is able to do far more

abundantly than all that we ask or think, according to the

power at work within us

Romans 15 :13 May the God of hope fill you with all joy

and peace as you trust in him, so that you may overflow

with hope by the power of the Holy Spirit.

Isaiah 56:6- Is not this the fast that I have chosen? to lose

the bands of wickedness, to undo the heavy burdens, and to

let the oppressed go free, and that ye break every yoke?

Isaiah 61:1 The spirit of the Lord is upon me because the

Lord hath anointed me to preach good tidings to the poor;

He has sent me to heal the brokenhearted, to proclaim

liberty to the captives, and the opening of the prison for

those who are bound .

About the Author

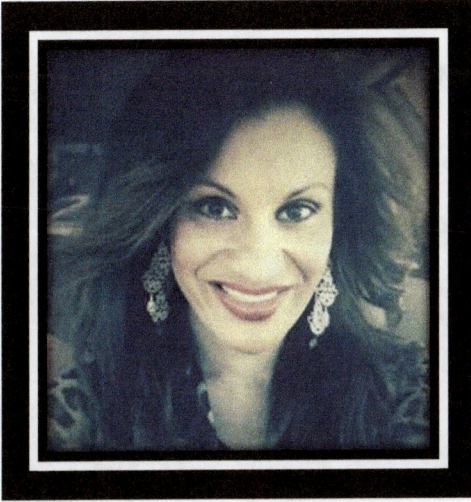

Jennifer A. Rosa is currently a student at California State University majoring in Psychology. Her minor is Child Development with an emphasis in Deaf Studies. Jennifer is passionate about wanting to see people delivered and set free from alcohol and drugs. She is the proud mother of three grown children and one grandson.